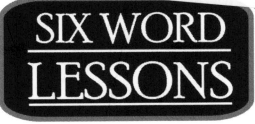

ON COPING WITH GRIEF

100 Lessons
to
Help You and Your Loved Ones
Deal with Loss

Shirley Enebrad
Over the Rainbow Bridge
Overtherainbowbridge.info

Six-Word Lessons on Coping with Grief – 6wordlessons.com
Editing by Patty Pacelli

Published by Pacelli Publishing
9905 Lake Washington Blvd. NE, #D-103
Bellevue, Washington 98004
Pacellipublishing.com

ISBN-10: 1-933750-33-2
ISBN-13: 978-1-933750-33-0

It has been said that we start the dying process as soon as we are born. Let's face it, no one gets to live forever. Each day an estimated 155,000 people die. That number creates two to ten times as many grievers.

I am a certified Grief Recovery Specialist with years of experience conducting grief workshops, retreats and support groups and I have personally dealt with many deaths. I am also the author of **Over the Rainbow Bridge, (My son's journey from here to Heaven)**, an inspiring book about my little boy's cancer journey.

In **Six-Word Lessons on Coping with Grief**, you will find 100 practical tips to help you navigate the depths of grief. I wrote this book to help you understand that you are not alone and your emotions experienced after the death of a loved one are not unique. There is no right or wrong way to grieve. There is no time limit. And most importantly, grieving is not a mental illness.

Everyone will grieve and most will experience many losses throughout his or her life. Loss covers deaths, job terminations, business closings, divorces and the end of friendships. For the purposes of **Six-Word Lessons on Coping with Grief**, I primarily address how to grieve a death. I have heard it all – the good, the bad, and the unhelpful. So, now it's time for useful information about grieving.

For more information, go to overtherainbowbridge.info or email me at enebrad@6wordlessons.com.

Mahalo,

Shirley

"Should you shield the canyons from the windstorms you would never see the true beauty of their carvings." --Dr. Elisabeth Kubler-Ross, Author, *On Death & Dying.*

For those who were left behind to mourn the following loved ones: Cory, John and Jesse Enebrad, Alycia Long Allen, Anne Geller, Ted Wilson, Henry Xu, Laura Friedman, Ryan Braykovich, Sparky Galando, Kathi Goertzen, Megan Bottman, Jessica Zemke and so many others. I hope this book helps bring perspective to your grief process. You are not alone.

A special mahalo to Lonnie and Patty Pacelli for your kokua in making this book possible.

Aloha nui loa to my family; Steven, Brie, Keili, Keawe, Keoni, Noel and Malia. We have survived countless windstorms and come out stronger for it.

Live aloha.

Table of Contents

You're Going to Grieve—Get Ready

1

Face it--you can't escape grief.

I was KO'd by the pain when my son died. So, I laced up the gloves, got in the ring and punched my way through the process. You must embrace the grief—not shut it out.

2

Shock--an emotional state of mind

Shock is a response to surprise endings such as death, divorce or termination. Your mind has to sort through what happened. I just put one foot in front of the other until the shock subsided. Just keep moving.

3

Numbness follows shock so be prepared.

When my seemingly healthy best friend died, numbness set in. I got stuck in neutral for days. I redirected my focus on the needs of her family. Do something good for others and yourself.

4

Denial is the next logical step.

Denial comes and goes. The brain's defense mechanism that says, "He isn't really gone . . . he is just away . . . it didn't really happen." I loved denial but I finally forced myself to choose reality. Wake up!

5

Anger isn't exclusively a male reaction.

I was angry when my mom died. She wore herself out caring for others. I didn't know whom I was angry with but I wanted to punch someone. Working out is safer and healthier so, get physical.

6

Sadness is a by-product of loss.

Sadness seeps in when the anger fades. I have suffered many losses, but hands down, the death of my child hurt most. I grieved his losses in addition to mine. Talking to someone helped. Start talking.

7

Fear creates anxiety and irrational thinking.

Fear of more losses and being plunged back into the depths of despair was overwhelming. I wrote down the reasons I was afraid. Acknowledging the fear reduced it tremendously. Face your fear.

8

Guilt can block healthy grief work.

No matter what, guilt happens. Why didn't . . . ? Woulda, Shoulda, Coulda. It's a distraction. You have to go through the grief to come out the other side. You cannot go around it, neither can you ignore or bury it with guilt. Let guilt go.

9

Hopeless and helpless-- a matched set

You may feel that your life will never be as it was before the loss. This leads to a sense that nothing can make your life better. This is what depression feels like. Focus on and believe in the future.

10

Acceptance is an island unto itself.

Acceptance takes time and energy. I fought this every step of the way. You don't want to accept what happened because it becomes another loss, the loss of your grief, which is your last connection to your loved one. Keep him in your heart.

Six-Word Lessons on Coping with Grief

There's No Right or Wrong Way

11

Nobody grieves the same as you.

I discovered that how we grieve is deeply personal. It is affected by our upbringing, belief system and our spirituality. Everyone is different. Our journeys are too. Try to understand and respect others' coping styles.

12

Grief's hard even for the healthy.

Everyone experiences many types of losses. The process is the same, but there is no pattern. Some steps repeat at the oddest times. A familiar song, face, or place can trigger a repeat step. The "Hey Kool-Aid" commercial was my undoing.

13

Crying doesn't mean you are weak.

"Tears heal the soul," said little Cory before he died. Crying is natural when grieving. It's a healthy response to physical or emotional pain and scientifically proven to reduce stress. Just grab a tissue and let 'em flow. I did.

14

Smiling doesn't mean you didn't care.

Give yourself a break. Grief fades with time. Don't beat yourself up about enjoying life again. You shouldn't feel badly about feeling good. My son asked that we celebrate his life not mourn his death. It made my grief easier.

15

Men are judged differently than women.

There are societal expectations put on men to be strong, do for others, and be the protector. They are busy stuffing emotions and doing their duties when they should be talking through their feelings. Talking and listening helps.

16

Women grieve openly and are supported.

Women heal by talking about their feelings. There's no stigma for crying. I surrounded myself and my daughter with supportive friends and family members and started a support group where we felt comfortable talking. Find someone to listen.

17

Young people's grief-- triggered by milestones

Children and teens have their own timetable and each milestone causes a whole new layer of grief issues. Workshops, camps and support groups give them outlets to express their feelings. I have seen miraculous awakenings.

18

Suicide causes an avalanche of emotions.

Suicide creates its own brand of guilt. When my sister's husband ended his life, the result was blame, guilt and anger that caused a family feud. Eventually emotions subsided. I listened, offered support and encouraged therapy.

19

Cultural differences and perceptions vary widely.

Each culture has death rituals and beliefs. Sometimes it's hard for others to understand. My son's nurse sounded the alarm, because according to her bias, we weren't crying enough, therefore we weren't grieving correctly. Don't judge.

20

Long term illness versus sudden death

Some grievers measure and compare their loss to others. I say, "Dead is dead and gone is gone. Long-term illness means your loved one dies a centimeter at a time. Sudden death means no goodbyes." Both are equally sad situations.

Guilt Will Get You Every Time

21

Guilt is tough
to deal with.

It gnaws at you. You feel awful and aim the anger or other emotions at yourself. It can cause feelings of shame and embarrassment, which makes it difficult to talk about, so you won't ask for help. Get the help you need.

22

Guilt might be based in reality.

You might feel that you weren't as supportive as you should have been. I examined every memory I could muster and beat myself up because of the things I didn't handle correctly. It made me feel worse.

23

Being nicer would have saved you.

If only you had been nicer to the person who died, then you wouldn't feel so terrible. Those "if only" thoughts are hard to shake. If you try, you can come up with many variations to help you feel inadequate. Don't do it.

24

No amount of time is enough.

Not spending enough time with a loved one prior to their death is classic. I bemoaned the fact that I chose not to go on a car trip with my grandfather years before he died. That was really reaching. Try to let it go.

25

Lack of appreciation lasts a lifetime.

If you tell yourself that you did not appreciate the person who died you can create a lifetime of reasons to be angry or embarrassed with yourself. Does that really help anyone? No, it just makes you feel worse. Stop it.

26

Your last contact was an argument.

This one is worse for those grieving a sudden death. You didn't know it was going to happen. Be kind to yourself. Try to focus on good memories. That's how I coped when my boyfriend died.

27

Hating the hospital visits and process

No one enjoys hospitals, witnessing gross procedures or a loved one's pain. Not wanting to be there doesn't mean you didn't care. I had no choice because I was a single mom but now I absolutely hate hospitals.

28

You didn't want to be there.

You had other things you wanted to do. This is a common issue for young people who resent the added chore of spending time with family members. Try to ignore the judging comments made by others who don't really know how you feel.

29

You should have pushed behavior changes.

So you did not insist that your loved one stop a self-destructive behavior such as smoking, alcohol or drug abuse. You did not cause the behavior. It was his or her choice. Give yourself a pass on this one.

30

Things you shouldn't have said aloud.

Words spoken in anger or frustration can haunt you forever. It happens to everyone. No one is perfect. It might help to write him or her an apology note. Don't let the guilt eat you alive.

Grief Affects You at Work Too

31

Grieving brains are like holey cheese.

Meetings at work were difficult. I was in a fog and my memory was like Swiss cheese for a few months. Please don't expect too much of yourself. Just roll with it. I swear it gets better eventually.

32

Work issues don't seem as important.

It was hard to focus on other people's wants and desires when I first got back to the grind. Nothing felt important enough for me to want to be there. My bad attitudes were born of emotion overload.

33

It's hard to concentrate at work.

I slept on the floor next to my son's bed for six weeks. I was physically and emotionally drained. It takes a while to get your strength back. Plus I was still vacillating between numbness, denial and pain.

34

Grief takes a toll on you.

Inability to sleep is a core issue, but irritability, impatience, and the need to self-soothe by any means possible (food, sex, substance use and withdrawal) will take a toll on your ability to function at home and work. Be aware.

35

Work might be place of refuge.

Some go back to work to escape from the reality of their loss. That doesn't mean it is easier there, but it helps to focus on outside issues. Guys like to "do" and women like to talk. Please be patient.

36

Routines sometimes help a griever focus.

The ability to focus is huge during the throes of grief. Getting back in the groove is a healthy distraction, but it won't stop the roller coaster or big wave slam from happening. Go with the flow.

37

Choose a supportive friend who listens.

When I needed to cry, I closed my office door and called my friend, Lynn. She listened without interruption or unsolicited advice. She cried with me. Having her friendship got me through the tough times.

38

Make sure that your boss understands.

Just about everyone has experienced the death of a loved one. Remind your boss how difficult loss is and if possible give him a sense of how you want to be treated by co-workers.

39

If anyone offers assistance--take it.

Take advantage of any assistance offered. Grief is not a mental illness. It's a direct response to loss. Short-term therapy can help. My therapist helped tremendously. Speak out loud.

40

Well-intentioned people make things worse.

Grievers talk about co-workers who offer platitudes and unsolicited advice. This is intrusive to those who want respite from their grief. Tell your boss if you don't want to talk about it at work.

Dealing With People's Insensitive Uninformed Comments

41

"I know how you must feel."

Some people want to relate to your situation in an effort to make you feel that you are not alone. This doesn't usually help much, so just nod and say "Maybe."

42

"He is in a better place."

People say this to try to comfort, believing that heaven truly is a better place—for the one who died. It will help you to remember that this person means well.

43

"The Lord doesn't give us more . . ."

It is overwhelming when dealing with the death of a loved one. Sometimes it does feel like more than one can handle. Ask for prayers of strength. Knowing that there are prayers being said can be a source of comfort.

44

"It all happened for the best."

This is often said about a stillbirth or SIDS. The person means well. It is painful but the only thing you can do in response is to nod and ignore this comment.

45

"Time to put this behind you."

Grievers make people uncomfortable. I am convinced that is why some say things without thinking. There is no timeline for grieving. Remember that there is no right or wrong way to grieve. It is what it is.

46

"At least he's out of pain."

A sincere person probably believes it when these words come out. It always made me feel selfish for wanting my son to still be alive even though he was sick. It's the words "at least" that hurt.

47

"If you think this is bad . . ."

This comment seemed to compare my son's death to something like a broken washing machine. This is usually spoken by someone who would rather talk about him or herself, so just try to brush it off and move on.

48

"Fortunately she had a long life."

My aunt was killed by a mentally ill street person. She was in great health. To grievers the age doesn't matter, their loved one's life was never long enough. Just grimace.

49

"You aren't over it yet? Why?"

This is another judgment about how you should be grieving, always imparted by someone who has never suffered a terrible loss. My reply was, "I will never be over *it*."

50

"Well, he did it to himself."

My aunt said this when my father died. When the deceased smoked, drank alcohol, used drugs or in Dad's case, refused dialysis, blaming creates distance from the deceased person. There are no words.

Six-Word Lessons on Coping with Grief

When It's Time for Talk Therapy

51

Throw the life ring, I'm drowning!

Of course a certain amount of sadness is unavoidable, but after awhile I felt overwhelmed and was drowning in my grief, so I got professional help. Grief specialists can help you move forward.

52

Talking about your feelings can help.

Luckily I am married to a psychologist, but even so, I highly recommend talk therapy. Grief is difficult to navigate. At times you feel a little crazy. An impartial person can reassure you.

53

Feeling like life isn't worth living

Complicated grief can morph into depression if you don't do the work. If you start feeling hopeless, listless and unwilling to take care of yourself, it is definitely time to seek professional help.

54

You wish you had died too.

This thinking is very common for parents when a child dies. If the feeling persists you should see a grief specialist or a therapist. I could not go there with this one because I had another child to raise.

55

You are beating yourself up unnecessarily.

One mom blamed her child's cancer on her pregnancy food choices and another thought allowing her child to see the movie *Ghostbusters* affected her immune system, causing the cancer. A support group helped both moms.

56

Feeling numb, disconnected and not yourself

Are you stuck? There's help. Talk to a friend, relative, pastor, support group, or therapist. I felt stuck after my friend died. My brothers came over and shook me. It worked.

57

Trusting others after loss is hard.

After the terrorist attacks of September 11, 2001, many of us could not trust. I got depressed seeing the video. We had been rocked to our foundation and our world was no longer safe. It's the same issue with death. It helps to verbalize it.

58

You are unable to function normally.

I didn't know how to be in a lopsided world after my son died. I floated out of my body and often felt as if I was on the outside looking in. My hope for normalcy returned with therapy.

59

Spending all of your effort grieving

I knew a mom who focused solely on her dead child. The family suffered because they lost both of them. She was afraid to live her life because it felt like betrayal. Therapy saved the family.

60

Letting go is worse than loss.

When you won't let go of your grief because it's your last connection to the dead person, you have to get some help. It doesn't have to be a therapist, but find someone to listen.

Make Time for Your Grief Work

61

Grief work is inevitable; don't delay.

Give yourself permission to grieve, then go for it. Grief is hard work, so attack it like any other work project. After all, it's your life. Recovering from grief takes concentration and dedication.

62

Many get religion in troubled times.

No matter what your beliefs, it might help you to speak with a religious person who could offer spiritual guidance. It doesn't have to be a clergy member. You could get comfort from many sources.

63

Knowledge is power and books deliver.

There are books that might give you what you need in terms of support, comfort or ideas of how to cope. I read books on spirituality, religious beliefs, and different cultures, sometimes just to take a break from my grief.

64

You need rest to grieve properly.

Make sure that you are eating healthy foods and getting enough rest. Neglecting either one is a sign of depression. So be aware of your emotions and moods and how they affect you. Take care of yourself.

65

Extreme behaviors can make grief worse.

If you over-indulge in food, alcohol, drugs, sex or sleep, you won't be able to do the work needed to get through grief. The sooner you face it the better. I took a few side trips but made it back.

66

Violent death and suicide add layers.

The dynamics change dramatically when the loss was caused by violence or was self-inflicted. Layers of guilt and tremendous anger are common reactions. Writing down your feelings or writing a letter to the perpetrator can help.

67

Signs of depression must be heeded.

Grief cannot kill you but depression can. The stress on your heart, brain and body should not be ignored. It is very important to take care of yourself. Stress causes cancer, heart attacks, strokes, etc. Deal with it.

68

Support groups are not for everyone.

You should try one. If you attend once to explore how it works, there is no pressure to participate, but you might like it and find it to be helpful. If you don't feel it's right, so be it, but at least give it a whirl.

69

Bopping 'til you drop is avoidance.

I have seen it and I have done it. I bopped until I hit the wall. Overloading yourself with activities causes a delay of your grief work. However, you will still have to do it so you may as well get it over with.

70

Believe in your ability to survive.

I read books like *The Power of Positive Thinking*. The first step to accomplishing anything is to believe that you can. It's true for surviving loss and making it to the other side of an ocean of scary emotions.

Don't Lose Sight of Others' Pain

71

Family members often struggle all alone.

When my mother died, our family grieved separately and selfishly. We all loved her. Don't get so caught up in your own stuff that you fail to notice that others might need your support and understanding.

72

Everyone's relationship was unique and special.

Some people might feel that their relationship with the deceased was more important than yours. Respect and honor your lost loved one's other relationships without getting sucked into the drama.

73

Broken families can cause more pain.

When my son died, my ex-in-laws behaved badly because of misinformation they had received. This made a horrible situation worse. Obviously they lost sight of what I had been through. Be kind.

74

Pay attention to children and teens.

Children and teens tend to hide their pain and delay grieving while watching their parents go through the process. If a child or teen is not eating or sleeping normally, is more irritable than usual or if grades slip, they need to talk to someone.

75

There's always one in every family.

Be prepared for disagreements and chaos when a family member dies. It tends to magnify if it is a parent and there is money involved. Try to maintain civility and be respectful of each other.

76

You must respect the deceased's wishes.

We had a huge brouhaha because two of my brothers were opposed to cremation even though that was our mother's wishes. Fighting compounds grief. Not everything is about you and your feelings. Be reasonable and respectful.

77

Be inclusive when making service plans.

When a family member dies it really helps to include everyone even if he or she didn't help before the death. There is much to do, so give everyone a role. It can prevent hurt feelings and unnecessary squabbles.

78

Divvy up belongings fair and square.

Nothing makes grieving harder than fighting with family members over "stuff." There are fair ways to handle this process. Remember that each person wants keepsakes and no one deserves more than the rest.

79

Memorialize your deceased loved one together.

Plan ways to honor your loved one together. Plant a tree or a garden, see their favorite musician, watch a favorite movie, feed the homeless at holiday time, or donate to causes in his or her name.

80

Celebrate the holidays with your family.

The first few years of holidays without your loved one at the table are the hardest. Get together with family and tell stories about the person you are all missing. Celebrate the times you shared.

Grief Changes but It Never Dies

81

Grief doesn't leave-- it just fades.

Unfortunately it's true, grief may last forever but it does fade with time. You just get used to the feelings and the fact that your loved one is gone. Accept the truth and move forward.

82

Ride out the waves of emotion.

No one ever gets over the loss, but you can get through the process. The intense emotions ebb and flow throughout the first few years. Ride it out and just believe that your life will get better.

83

Now put away that stupid stopwatch.

There is no time limit. Grief can take weeks, months or years. Give yourself ample time, and remind yourself of the value of grieving well. Look forward to when it isn't the most important part of your life.

84

Prayers do work
for most things.

Spiritual activities like praying, attending church or temple or meditating are healthy ways to work through grief. Grief often causes questions of faith, so it could be a good time to talk to clergy or explore other religions or beliefs.

85

Creative expression can nurture your growth.

Painting a work of art is a great way to express loss. Writing about your feelings is also a powerful coping mechanism as it allows you to externalize the emotions, fears, sadness and eventual acceptance that you feel while grieving.

86

Music therapy promotes healing from grief.

When looking at the options for teens or anyone in mourning, consider the use of music therapy. Grievers are encouraged to write songs about your emotions. I had workshop participants write poetry and songs to express their feelings.

87

Moving through grief doesn't mean forgetting.

Your loved one would want you to go on and live your life, to be happy and productive. Don't let his death cause you to stop living your life. Honor his memory through the experiences you have and the people whose lives you touch.

88

Accept help when it is offered.

You may need to find new ways of doing things, make lifestyle changes, or engage in self-growth and exploration. Be sure to accept help when it is offered. It will help both you and the helper. People want to help, they just don't know how. Let them.

89

Take all the time you need.

Don't make any big decisions right after a loss. Making financial decisions or other major plans while grieving is a bad idea. You might regret such decisions later when you are in a healthier state of mind with better judgment. Stay put until you are completely sure.

90

When the fog lifts you'll see.

Moving on does not mean that you will forget your loved one, it just means that you will replace the pain with special memories. Let him or her go. Cherish the memories. You won't forget.

Keeping the Memories Alive--Moving on

91

Memories, like grief, fade with time.

My memories began to fade, which made me feel guilty. It's not possible to cling to every shared moment. This is normal and inevitable. I kept journals and a scrapbook to help restore memories later. Then, I wrote a book.

92

Although it hurts, life goes on.

It feels like yesterday. I haven't forgotten him. The hole in my heart and the pain are still there, but I just got used to it. You'll learn to adapt and go on too. You won't be leaving him or her behind. Live again.

93

Write letters to your loved one.

Sometimes you just need to get your feelings down on paper. This really can help you feel better, especially if you still have guilt or unfinished business to process. I write letters and then burn them.

94

Make a timeline of your life.

I have workshop participants do this one. It helps to put your life in perspective on paper. Start with birth and end with present day. Chronicle the good times and the bad ones. My first one helped me see the balance.

95

Cleaning out the closet takes courage.

When it is time to clean out the closet or drawers of your lost loved one, make a clear plan. You cannot keep it all. Choose a few favorites for yourself, and sort the rest into piles—one for giving to the appropriate people, and one for donating to charity. Remember, it's just stuff.

96

Holidays and special dates are challenging.

Sometimes, I could feel myself getting down about a month before special dates. Try to keep busy and focus on good memories. Just know that it is normal to experience down times for a few years around the holidays, birthdays and anniversaries.

97

Include them when celebrating special days.

I knew someone who pretended that her dead child never existed. This can result in disaster. Celebrate birthdays and remember him or her at Christmas and encourage others to do the same. He or she deserves to be remembered, but don't go to the other extreme either.

98

Share organized photos and keepsakes regularly.

If you have children or teens it is important to keep the memories of your loved one alive for them too. Create memory books together using the photos and keepsakes. Give the books a place of prominence and share often.

99

Give special meaning to her life.

My in-laws created an arts center memorial fund to honor their daughter. I helped children with cancer for my son. Creating a legacy gives meaning to the lives of our loved ones so, donate, plant a tree, or get involved with a cause.

100

In the end, love sustains you.

Goodbyes hurt, but laughter lowers blood pressure and stress. So, remember the good times, have gratitude for the time you had. Celebrate life. Forget the regrets. Laugh often. Live well, and remember that love never dies.

See the entire Six-Word Lesson Series at
6wordlessons.com

Want to learn more about
coping with grief?
Contact Shirley at
enebrad@6wordlessons.com

Read more about Shirley at
Overtherainbowbridge.info